Building Memories

Planning a Meaningful Cremation Funeral

by Doug Manning

In-Sight Books

September 2002

Copyright© 2002 by In-Sight Books, Inc.
P. O. Box 42467
Oklahoma City, Oklahoma 73123
800.658.9262 or 405.810.9501
www.insightbooks.com

Manufactured in the United States of America

ISBN 1-892785-43-9

Cover Photo:
Ted West Photography, Oklahoma City, Oklahoma

W hen I die ⌒
I want my funeral to provide reality,
memories,
and permission to grieve
to my family.

> For in those three things there is
> healing
> and my prayer is that,
> above all,
> *the family will be drawn into*
> *a closer bond of love.*
> *because,*

A death in the family either bonds or it
divides the family relationships.

> If the family is helped,
> and the bond is strengthened,
> *then I have had the best of funerals*

⌒ *Doug Manning*

The Family Facing a Loss

When a loved one dies the family must make some very hard decisions while under tremendous stress. Emotions are in a state of upheaval, and feelings so tender the slightest misunderstanding can become a major issue.

Some families have maintained a close enough relationship that they know how each member of the family responds to such times. Other families have not had the chance to spend a great deal of time together and must make these decisions with family members that are almost strangers to each other.

Over the years I have observed that families can become divided at times like this and those divisions can last for years. This guide was written to help your family face this loss with unity and love.

Since cremation has been chosen and, quite possibly, there will be those in the family who have never been involved in this kind of disposition of the body, it becomes even more imperative that we proceed with care.

The First Step is to Have a Family Meeting

Usually one or two people will be looked upon as the leaders in this family decision. These people should find a time and place where just the immediate family can have a meeting without interruptions. The funeral home, or a church can offer such a place for this meeting. If no other place can be found, a back bedroom can suffice if arrangements are made for no one to interrupt the meeting. Phone calls can be returned later and friends can wait while this vital meeting takes place. This is a perfect opportunity for that special friend who wants to help in some way to be at the house to field phone calls and meet people who come to call.

Far too often the family never has a private time together throughout the whole funeral process. They need time alone to express their grief to each other as well as this time of planning.

When the group is together someone should take this planning guide and walk through each question in order. This leads to a full discussion of the major points and hopefully leads to a sense of unity in planning. No one should feel like they were not consulted nor heard.

The Number One Priority Must be Family Unity

This must take precedence over our own desires. It must take precedence over established traditions. At times we must even put the unity of the family above the desires and plans expressed by the deceased. We will want to do as much as possible to meet the requests of our loved one, but we must have the freedom to change anything that is necessary for the good of the family. The most important concern is for the family to come through this time with togetherness and peace.

Pre-Planning a Funeral

If this guide is used in pre-planning a funeral there is still a need for a family meeting. Use this guide in the same manner to walk the family through this meeting.

I have always loved the story of an elderly gentleman who had burial plots on both coasts. The family kept after him to tell them where he wanted to be buried. He thought for a moment and then said, "Surprise me." We walk a fine line between knowing what we want to happen at our own funeral and forcing some hard decisions on our family. Conditions change, situations become altered and suddenly the family cannot fulfill all of the requests we have made. Many a family lives with long-term guilt over failing a loved one in this area.

The answer to this is to make general plans, have a family meeting so everyone has a voice in the plans and understands what is to happen, and then make it clear that it will be all right if changes have to be made.

I cannot emphasize enough that family unity is priority number one. The only way to avoid misunderstanding is to have an understanding. A family discussion is in order.

Question One
What About Cremation?

Cremation is the method of choice for a growing number of families in the United States and Canada. It can be a very meaningful and beautiful form of caring for the body of a loved one. Cremation should be looked upon as simply an alternative to burial. I personally react when someone says, "We are *just* going to have him cremated." This suggests that cremation is somehow a second rate or easier form of burial and that it is done to avoid hassle or to save time. Cremation is not an inferior alternative in any way. The family who chooses this form of care for a loved one should never feel any sense of not doing the best nor caring as much for a loved one.

As a minister I am often asked if there is anything in the Bible that indicates how we should feel about cremation. I must say that to my knowledge there is no position on cremation at all though some religious doctrines have strict guidelines about cremation. My only advice to families is that cremation should not take away from the funeral ceremonies that have been proven as healing. Nor should cremation deny members of the family the right to view the body if that is something they find meaningful.

I have spoken in New Zealand where eighty percent of the funerals are followed by cremation. Because of the widespread acceptance there, they have established definite ceremonies for these services. There is no difference in the cremation service and the burial service except that in the cremation service the family comes forward at the close of a service and lays flowers on the casket in a time of closure and saying good-bye. Often, family members will say a few words on these occasions. The person leading the service will then have a ceremony of committal similar to those used at the grave side in the cemetery. Ceremony is a vital part of the healing process in grief, and they have developed ceremonies that fit their culture.

Unfortunately, we have not had the time to develop these ceremonies here in North America. That is why this guide was written. Our hope is that this guide will help your family plan a ceremony that honors your loved one and fits your family.

This guide is not designed to talk you out of cremation, nor sell you anything, nor "upgrade" any choices you make. The hope of the author is that it will simply share the options with you with simplicity and clarity so you can make choices that will be good for your family.

When my brother, Tom, died no one explained all of the choices and options we had. Tom was immediately cremated without anyone seeing him after he died. A few days later we had a memorial service that was designed to deny that anyone had died. We thought that was the norm if cremation was used. We had no idea that we could depart from the norm. We missed the chance for coming together as a family. We missed the chance to use the funeral to establish the significance of my brother. In the process we trivialized his life and his death. Regret over that led me to write this guide to help people know about the options and choices. We start by exploring the value of the funeral.

Question Two
Why Have a Funeral?

Most of us have never confronted that question. Funerals seem to be a necessary evil we endure when someone in the family dies. Now you are called upon to make decisions about the kind of funeral you want for a loved one. I have put together some thoughts on the value of the funeral for you to consider.

When bad things happen to us the first thing we want and need to do is establish the significance of the event. Friends of Jacqueline Kennedy were shocked when, almost immediately after the President's assassination, she compulsively asked people, "Do you want to hear about it?" and rattled off each frame of that terrible sequence in her soft, shaken voice. She had to share the experience. That is establishing significance and it is human nature.

We see the same reaction when someone has surgery or has recovered from an illness. There is an almost insatiable need to talk about the surgery or the illness. We need to talk in order to work through the significance the event has had on our lives.

When I discovered the need for significance I began to understand the vital importance of the funeral. When someone we love has died, the ceremonies and the funeral process establish the significance of the person and the significance their lives have had in our lives. If we can establish significance, we can move on; if we can't, then grief and grieving become a much more difficult and delayed process.

We really know all of this instinctively. A few days after the Oklahoma City bombing I was asked to write materials to help the families whose loved ones would not be found and identified or whose loved ones could not be viewed by the family. After the tragic events of September 11, 2001, once again I wrote a small book for the families who lost loved ones in the World Trade Center, Pentagon and airplanes involved in the attack. The professionals working each of these disasters knew that the pain would be made much worse for those families who were deprived of this vital part of the grieving process.

We know inside ourselves that we need to have a time of reality and mourning when someone dies. I call that process establishing the significance of the loss.

The Funeral and Significance

The funeral process establishes significance. That is what the funeral is for and that is the value of the funeral process. The whole funeral experience helps establish significance in two meaningful areas.

Personal Significance

First we must establish the personal significance of the person who has died. We need to discover how important our loss is before we can grieve it. This is necessary because we really do not know the value of a person until they are gone. I have loved my wife for over forty years. When she had emergency bypass surgery and I had to face the fact that I might lose her, I found value in her that day that I never knew existed. I still do not know her total value, and will not, unless she dies first. We do not know what we have lost until we have lost it. That is why we must establish the significance this person had in our lives before we can move on in our recovery.

Planning a funeral is an act of love. Some folks have tried to paint the funeral as plastic, costly, meaningless and even pagan. They seem to think the sophisticated thing to do is deny death and ignore the inner need to express love toward a loved one who has died.

I had the privilege of planning the funerals for both of my parents. My father, like most fathers, said he did not want us to go to any trouble, that we should just put him in an old pine box and throw him in a ditch somewhere. I told him the funeral was my gift of love to him and that I would make the decisions about the size and nature of this gift. He was most pleased to hear that. He did not want an old pine box, but thought he was supposed to say he did.

I picked out a casket that fit each of my parents. Mother would have loved the colors and I needed the act of love involved in the planning. I planned the music, the people who would sing or speak and designed the service to be very personal. As I did the planning, I was internalizing the value and significance these people had in my life.

Gatherings provide a chance to talk. Visitation times at the funeral home or friends dropping by the home give us the chance to begin telling the stories about our loved one. We establish significance as we talk about the person. The stories we tell will one day become the great memories that stay in our hearts forever.

The funeral gives us permission to grieve. Our society seems to see grief as an enemy to be avoided. We seem to think that respected people do not show grief in public. Several years ago, an article in a magazine described what the author thought was the barbarian practice of having a "three-hanky funeral" as if that was the ultimate in poor taste. The implication is that brave and cultured people do not cry or express their emotions. They are to carry their heads high and never show any sign of cracking. Somehow we developed the idea that grief is hard on the family and should be avoided if at all possible. Sometimes families choose not to have a funeral with the idea that if they do not have that final experience, they will not grieve as much.

Grief is not an enemy. It is nature's way of healing a broken heart. We are doing the best job of handling grief when we are grieving. The more we express our grief the sooner we work through this process that leads to health. Nothing that I know of gives us a better chance and more freedom of expression than the funeral experience.

Social Significance

We also need to establish the social significance of the person. That is what the funeral is all about. A funeral is a gathering of family and friends to establish the significance of a life. It is designed to say to the family that this life mattered to them and to the friends who were also touched by this life.

When my grandmother died, I was overwhelmed by the flowers in the church. Each flower said this dear lady was important to someone. I will never forget that sight. Nor will I ever forget what comfort it was to me to know how significant she was to others. To this day I love flowers at funerals. It has become a trend to request that a donation be made in lieu of flowers. I give to charities on other occasions, but when friends lose a loved one, I want them to know that their loss is significant and that their loved one mattered.

Significance is best established when a funeral focuses on the life of the person. We are now learning the value of personalizing the funeral for this purpose. Families now feel free to eulogize their loved one, or to ask a close friend to do so. Many families bring personal items and pictures to the service to further personalize the event. Music is now more likely to be a song the person loved or a song that meant a great deal to a marriage.

If I could do it over again, I would have planned a service for my brother that personalized his life. The service we had was more of an effort to avoid facing his death. My mother sat through the service without shedding a tear. We thought we had produced a funeral that was easy on the family. Several years later I still have a problem with my lack of closure and the lack of time spent establishing what Tom meant to me. Without that opportunity to openly grieve our loss, we have had a hard time moving on toward healing.

The funeral is not about caskets and rituals. The funeral is about mental health and healing. When we have inventoried our loss and begun the healing process of grief, then, and only then, has the funeral done its vital work in our lives.

Question Three
Should We View the Body?

Often it is assumed that if cremation is to be used, then there can not be any viewing of the loved one. There is no basis for this assumption at all. Cremation does not change anything except the final disposition of the body of a loved one. Any wish a family might have can be done in a cremation service just as it can in burials. To prepare the body for viewing before cremation is no different than preparing the body before burial and both have the same therapeutic effect on the family.

While I am a great believer in the value of the family seeing the body, every family must make that choice for themselves. If the choice is made not to view, then I recommend that the family find other ways to face the reality of the loss. I counsel far too many families who did not face the visual reality of their loss and, as a result, suffer from delayed and internalized grief. Preparing the body for viewing by the family adds some cost to the funeral, but embalming is a small percentage of the funeral cost. The funeral director will be most happy to show you the actual additional cost of this service.

Viewing can be the first step in a healthy grieving experience. This may seem like a terrible ordeal to put a grieving person through, but it is hard to find reality without it. It may seem difficult, but in most cases it has a healing and comforting effect on us. Our last view of a loved one alive is often not the one we want to carry the rest of our lives. After my father died, I was so relieved to see him peaceful, instead of gasping for one last breath when he was dying.

Our efforts to avoid viewing often leave far too much to the imagination. Imagination will always make it worse than it was in reality. My former business associate did not get to see her son who died of suicide. Months later she got the pictures the police took of the scene and told me the pictures were so much better than her imagination had made it seem to her. As a grief counselor, I have seen how much solace this can provide a family, and how little is then left to the imagination. This is especially true after a death following an illness. We often hear folks say they wish to remember the person as they were. That is fine if we did not have to see them while they were desperately ill.

Of course there are reasons not to have the body viewed. Some people have a problem viewing the bodies of others who have died and have no desire for theirs to be seen. Most of the time they will say it is all right for the family to view, but they do not want to have an open casket at the funeral. Viewing is a personal choice and the casket being open at a funeral is always left to the family's discretion.

It is important for your family to feel free to decide how they want the service. If they wish to have the body lovingly prepared for viewing before cremation, that is available. If they wish the body to be viewed by family members only, that is their choice. If they wish no viewing whatsoever, that is also a family choice.

The First Rule in Funerals is—
There Are No Rules ⌒

If a song has meaning to the family or the person
it should be sung.

If there are special people who can share
meaningful thoughts and insights into the life of
the person
they should be heard.

If the family wants to speak
they should do so even if their voices
break and they must stop for a
cry or so.

If there are special things that had meaning
to the person: a fishing boat, an old car,
pictures of the life, mementos of an occupation …
they should be at the service.

These are the things that make a
funeral meaningful.

Feel free to express and honor without rules ⌒

Question Four
What Type of Service Fits Our Family?

We can forget cremation for a moment and decide what type of service you want. There is no reason for cremation to enter into this picture. Utilizing cremation does not put any limits whatsoever on what can be done at the funeral. Examples would be:

- Full traditional or contemporary service before your loved one has been cremated with the body present at the service.

- Full service before cremation with loved one not present.

- Memorial service after cremation has taken place.

- Any combination of the above.

The choices are unlimited. Every family should feel free to choose exactly what they want.

Question Five
What Kind of Gatherings Will Be Meaningful?

Visitations at the funeral home or people gathering in your home have great meaning. Too often these are forgotten when cremation is to be used. We seem to think that if the body is not at the funeral home, then there is no reason for the family and friends to go there. In many cases, of course, the body is there. As discussed earlier, there is no reason why a body cannot be prepared for viewing at a visitation and then be cremated. It is no more illogical to do that before cremation than it is to do it before burial.

Cremation should not have any bearing on the gatherings. The family needs the presence of friends during this trying time. Most of the help you will receive during this time of grief will come from your friends. Gatherings provide a great time to talk about the loss. This meets the need to establish the social significance of the person.

The funeral home provides a quiet and restful setting for these gatherings. The family home can become quite chaotic during the days of mourning. It is a wonderful respite to go to the funeral home for an uninterrupted time with friends and family.

Question Six
Who Should Participate?

With the modern day equipment now available, pallbearers are not a necessity at any funeral. We choose them to honor their friendship. We choose them because their presence is a source of comfort to us. We choose them because their presence is part of establishing the social significance of the person. Cremation should not have any effect on this choice. It is appropriate for the family to choose pallbearers even if the body is not present for any of the funeral processes. The need for friends to be with us never changes with the type of the funeral. When cremation is used, the pallbearers serve as an honored escort instead of carrying the casket.

Having friends or family members taking part in the tribute by sharing a story, performing a song, or lighting candles as part of a closing ceremony, all add great meaning and will be a cherished part of the memory of the service.

If the family makes a list of the participants the funeral home can usually contact the people for you. Many families find it meaningful to contact these people themselves. Often one person needs some involvement and will be more than happy to make these calls. There is a space in the back of this planning guide for you to list those you wish to serve in these positions.

Question Seven
How Can We Make the Service Personal?

The major complaint lodged against funerals, and one of the reasons people choose not to have a funeral, is the lack of personalization. Far too often, all funerals seem to be the same. If the goal is to establish significance, then making each funeral personal becomes a necessity. A funeral should be unique to the person being honored. This can be accomplished in many ways, and can be accomplished without the family having to burden themselves with time-consuming thinking and activity when they are already overwhelmed. Personalization involves:

Choice of Speakers

Funerals With Clergy

Normally a clergy person is called to officiate at the funeral. Usually the family has some attachment to a church or knows a clergy person to call. Many families find the words of comfort found in their faith to be an invaluable help in this time of need.

Often it is helpful to have additional participants in the service. A close friend telling the wonderful stories seems to establish the significance of the life and your loss like nothing else can.

When the families do not belong or attend a church they often feel like they are imposing if they ask a clergy person to officiate at the service. Your funeral director may have a list of clergy he or she calls on when needed.

Funerals Without Clergy

A funeral does not have to be religious. The church does not have some kind of exclusive claim to the ceremonies of remembrance we need to experience. It is most proper to have a funeral without the services of a clergy person. A good friend, someone who likes to do public speaking or even family members can do a great job of making the funeral meaningful. When my mother died we chose to have just the family speak, and I think we did a wonderful job of honoring her memory. There are now Certified Celebrants© in many parts of the country who are specifically trained to provide beautiful personalized services. Your funeral director can tell you if there is a Celebrant available in your area.

Music

For many people, music is the most important and meaningful part of any service. Most of us have songs that hold very special meaning for us. These can be songs we love to hear, or whose lyrics have special meaning for us, or songs that meant a great deal to a marriage or friendship. If at all possible, these songs should be sung at the funeral. Some churches have rules concerning the music that can be used in the church, but funeral homes have no such rules and usually can find the songs requested. I spent two days looking for "Red Sails in the Sunset" a few years ago. After I heard what the song had meant to the couple, I thought the time was well spent.

The music can be performed live with a singer or many people choose to use CDs by the original artist and even put together a medley of favorite songs.

There are no rules about the number of songs to be used in a service. The only limit is time. If a person was a great lover of music, then it is appropriate to fill a great portion of the service with music. I hope my funeral is done with much singing and very little talking.

Pictures

Families are often now encouraged to bring pictures for display at the funeral. The gathering and choosing of the pictures is a great time for establishing significance and usually starts the family reminiscing and sharing the worth of the person. The arranging of the display can be an act of love that has a great deal of meaning for those who perform the task. In every case I have ever seen, the pictures were tremendously important to those who came to the funeral. A picture display can be easily arranged by simply telling the funeral director of your wishes. Designate one person to head up the picture project. That person should enlist as many others as possible, but it helps to have one person in charge.

With computer technology it is now possible to scan pictures and combine them with music utilizing Power Point or other software programs. This makes a wonderful tribute that can be shown at visitation or during the funeral. Ask your funeral director if that is an option.

Personal Items

A friend of mine loved to refurbish old Model A cars and John Deere tractors. At his funeral we parked one of each on the sidewalk outside the church. The presence of the car and tractor said a great deal about the person, it said a great deal about how much we loved the person, and it became a way of starting conversations and stories from his friends. We came home with new perspective on his life and great memories to keep.

I have seen fishing boats, wood work, hand work, quilts, paintings and so many other items I cannot begin to list them all, shared at funeral services. Each item has a place of honor for family and friends.

Humor

If no one is going to laugh at my funeral, I am not going to attend. Laughter has been such a part of my life that no one could ever memorialize me without it. I have told many funny stories at funerals. There are just times when that is the only way to express who the person was. Some of the most personal and comforting funerals I have performed have been those in which I have dared to tell these kinds of stories.

Receptions

The one problem I have always had with cremation funerals is that there is no feeling of completion at the end of the service. The friends just file out and go home. There is no way to offer support and love like we do when we gather at the cemetery. I have sat in the parking lots of funeral homes and wondered what to do next after these services.

Some people now have receptions after the service. These need not be long or elaborate. Tea and coffee are refreshments enough, though some families also serve cookies or cake. This provides a wonderful time for the friends to tell the family how much the person means to them. And we once more meet the idea of a funeral being a time to establish and share the significance of the person who has died. Some funeral homes now have reception rooms and catering services to meet the growing need for this important time of gathering. Most churches have a reception hall or community room that can be used for this purpose.

Question Eight
What Choices do We Need to Make?

Most of the choices you need to make are already determined by the type of funeral you have planned. There are some options that still need addressing.

Obituary

The family will need to collect the dates and information for an obituary. This will vary from city to city. Some newspapers allow the family to write their own obituaries, while others ask for just the bare facts and obituaries are written by their staff. Your funeral director will know the local customs.

An obituary consists of all the pertinent dates such as birth, death, marriage, when the person moved to the area. It also should list any affiliations such as church, civic clubs and social groups. It is appropriate to tell the occupation of the person, and certainly we should list activities that define the life of our loved one. If they were active in a church or a charity, or if they volunteered for some cause, this should be included.

The funeral director will take your information, add the details of the service and submit the obituary to the media.

Often the family must face delicate issues in preparing obituaries. Such things as former mates, partners who are not yet married and all the other possibilities that exist in our society. My opinion is that the best way to handle these situations is to be as up-front as possible without being obtrusive. If a person is living with someone, then list that person as a special friend or a significant other. If there are former mates involved, list them as the mother or father of the surviving children. Trying to avoid saying what everyone already knows leaves us looking foolish. Society does not look upon these issues in the same way it once did and we should feel free to be honest about the person's life.

Caskets

If you have chosen to have an opportunity for viewing during visitation, at the funeral, or privately with the family, then the selection of a casket is one of the decisions that will need to be made.

In my experience with families, the choosing of a casket can have a great deal of meaning. The casket, the clothes, the way the hair is combed and the cosmetics used can all become a way of expressing love and that final opportunity to care for the person.

The funeral home has a wide range of caskets, some of which are specially designed for cremation. These caskets are built with a minimum of metal and are of materials that will be consumed more thoroughly. There are containers and caskets of many types made from several kinds of materials. The family should consult with the funeral director and select what you think fits your situation and the type of service you have planned.

Final Rest

There has been a change in thinking about the final resting place for the ashes. Scattering the ashes in some favorite place or from an airplane is no longer as popular as it once was. Families probably need to think this through very carefully before they take this action. Once it is done, there is no turning back. It sounds almost romantic, but families need to understand that the reality is not quite what they expected. The remains are not just ash. There is some solid matter left after cremation and if families do not know what to expect, they can find this quite disturbing.

We are discovering that families need a place where their loved one is remembered and a place to connect to their roots. A visit to the Vietnam Memorial will convince anyone of the importance of a place to be remembered. One of the actions Hitler took when he overtook Poland was to dig up the cemeteries. He wanted to eliminate their history thus destroying them as a people, and he understood the devastation of losing that part of their identity.

If the ashes are to be scattered, then a family should consider keeping some of the ashes for burial. Many families choose to bury the ashes in the plot already occupied by other family members. Some place the ashes in a columbarium. Some families purchase an urn and keep the ashes with them at home. There are now sharing urns which are small urns into which a small portion of the ashes can be stored so each family member can have one.

If it is not possible to retain some of the ashes, then perhaps the family can find an appropriate place to memorialize the loved one. Establishing a garden, purchasing a bench or planting a tree are some ways that families have made "a place to remember".

Funeral directors have a wide variety of urns to fit the family's needs. These range from the more decorative urns designed to remain in the home to those more appropriate for burial. The family should take some time in deciding on the type of final rest and type of urn.

After the Planning is Done, It is Time for Family Stories

I hope the plans are now made and the family is satisfied with the decisions that have been made. While you are all together, may I suggest a time of family story telling?

The night before my grandmother's funeral, my father said, "Let's go down and visit Mama Hoyle." We went to the funeral home, sat beside her casket and spent a couple of hours telling Mama Hoyle stories. I shall never forget the night. We broke through the barriers families build to keep from sharing grief with each other. We started a tradition that night that continues to this day. Anytime my family gets together, we tell those same stories. I not only know what stories will be told, I know the order in which they will be told. Because of this story telling, Mama Hoyle is still alive among us. No one is dead until they are forgotten. She is not dead.

Because that night meant so much to me, I get families together the night before the funeral for this kind of story telling. These sessions are always special. Most of the time the stories are funny. I especially like to have these sessions with the body present. It is like the person is with us and enjoying each story.

I also like to do these sessions when the person is old and has died after a long illness. Recently we had a session with an old man who had Alzheimer's disease. His personality had died years before, but that night he came back to life among us as we remembered all the stories. All the funeralizing doesn't happen at the funeral.

Personal Information

Name: _____

Birthdate: _____ Birthplace: _____

Social Security Number: _____

Current Address: _____

_____

Resident Since: _____ Citizen of: _____

Phone: _____ Marital Status: _____

Occupation: _____

Previous Occupation: _____

Education

School: _____

Dates Attended: _____

Diploma/Degree: _____

Military Service

Branch: _____ Rank: _____

Date of Enlistment: _____ Date of Discharge: _____

Serial Number: _____

Fraternal, Service & Union Memberships:

_____

_____

_____

Special Recognitions/Honors:

_____

_____

_____

Community Service:

_____

_____

_____

Parents/Spouse/Partner:

Father's Name: _____ Birthdate: _____

   Birthplace: _____ Date of Death: _____

Mother's Name: _____ Birthdate: _____

   Birthplace: _____ Date of Death: _____

Spouse/Partner's Name: _____ Birthdate: _____

   Birthplace: _____ Date of Death: _____

Children:

Name: _____ Birthdate: _____

    Birthplace: _____

    Current Address: _____

    Spouse: _____

    Children: _____

Name: _____ Birthdate: _____

    Birthplace: _____

    Current Address: _____

    Spouse: _____

    Children: _____

Name: _____ Birthdate: _____

    Birthplace: _____

    Current Address: _____

    Spouse: _____

    Children: _____

Name: _____ Birthdate: _____

    Birthplace: _____

    Current Address: _____

    Spouse: _____

    Children: _____

The Funeral

Funeral Home/Funeral Director

_____ Phone _____

Cemetery/Mausoleum

_____ Phone_____

Burial _____ Location of Plot _____

Cremation _____

Disposition of Ashes:

Buried _____

Scattered _____

Shared _____

Casket/Urn Choice _____

Location of Services _____

Persons Involved in the Service

Clergy/Celebrant _____

Family_____

Friends _____

Pall Bearers _____

_____

_____

Type of Service

Church Service _____

Military Service _____

Lodge Service _____

Other _____

Music _____

_____

_____

_____

_____

Pictures _____

_____

_____

_____

_____

Readings _____

_____

_____

_____

_____

Viewing _____

_____

Stories _____

_____

_____

_____

Flowers _____

_____

_____

_____

Special Requests _____

_____

_____

_____

Reception/Gathering _____

_____

_____

_____

Donations/Charities _____

_____

_____

_____

Important Documents

Location & Contacts

Indicate the location of each list or document that is applicable or the person responsible for it.

Will/Trust Documents _____

_____

Birth Certificate _____

_____

Marriage Certificate _____

_____

Divorce Decree _____

_____

Veteran's Discharge Certificates _____

_____

Social Security Card _____

_____

Insurance Policies _____

_____

Retirement Benefits Documents _____

_____

Automobile Title(s) _____

_____

Deeds to Real Estate _____

_____

List of Utilities & Account Numbers _____

_____

List of Telephone & Computer Services & Account Numbers _____

_____

List of Credit Cards & Account Numbers _____

_____

List of Financial Institutions, account numbers & types of account

_____

Stock Certificates/Bonds _____

_____

Income Tax Returns _____

_____

Cemetery/Funeral Arrangement Documents _____

_____

Safe Deposit Key _____

_____

(Note: documents that might be needed immediately after a death should not be kept in a safe deposit box as they may be needed at a time when banking institutions are closed.)

Other Important Documents: _____

_____

Doug Manning

His career has included minister, counselor, business executive, author and publisher. He and his wife, Barbara, have been parents to four daughters and long-term caregivers to three parents.

After thirty years in the ministry, Doug began a new career in 1982. He now devotes his time to writing, counseling and leading seminars in the areas of grief and elder care. His publishing company, In-Sight Books, Inc., specializes in books, video and audio tapes specifically designed to help people face some of the toughest challenges of life.

Doug has a warm, conversational style in which he shares insights from his various experiences. Sitting down to read a book from Doug is like having a long conversation with a good friend.

Selected Resources from In-Sight Books

Don't Take My Grief Away From Me
The Gift of Significance—Walking With People Through a Loss
The Special Care Series
Lean On Me Gently—Helping the Grieving Child
Thoughts for the Lonely Nights journal and CD
Thoughts for the Grieving Christian journal and CD
Thoughts for the Holidays—Finding Permission to Grieve

For a complete catalog or ordering information, contact:

In-Sight Books

800.658.9262 or 405.810.9501
www.insightbooks.com
orders&info@insightbooks.com